ANC ... MER

Franklin Watts
Published in Great Britain in 2016 by The Watts Publishing Group

Copyright © Franklin Watts 2015

Editor: Sarah Ridley
Editor in Chief: John C. Miles
Series designer: John Christopher/White Design
Art director: Peter Scoulding
Picture research: Diana Morris

A CIP catalogue record for the book is available from the British Library.

Dewey number: 935
ISBN 978 1 4451 3400 0

Printed in China

Franklin Watts
An imprint of
Hachette Children's Group
Part of The Watts Publishing Group
Carmelite House
50 Victoria Embankment
London EC4Y 0DZ

An Hachette UK Company
www.hachette.co.uk

www.franklinwatts.co.uk

Picture credits
© Album/Oronoz/Superstock: 14; © The Art Archive/Alamy: front cover, 1, 5, 20;
© Ashmolean Museum, University of Oxford/Bridgeman Art Library: 13b; © Bettmann/
Corbis: 7; © De Agostini/Getty Images: 21; © De Agostini/Superstock: 16, 17; © Giraudon/
Bridgeman Art Library: 18; © Hardnfast/CC Wikipedia Commons: 22; © Iberfoto/
Superstock: 28; © Iraq Museum, Baghdad/Photo Scala, Florence: 12; © Kmiragaya/
Dreamstime: 15; © Erich Lessing/AKG Images: 8, 25, 27; © Clay McLachlan: 9t; © Gianni
d'agli Orti/Corbis: 26b; © The Print Collector/Alamy: 13t; © Zev Radovan/Bridgeman
Art Library: 6; © Walter Rawlings/Robert Harding PL: 24, 29; © Nico Tondini/Robert
Harding PL: 23; © Wikimedia: 10, 11, 26t.

*Every attempt has been made to clear copyright. Should there be any inadvertent omission
please apply to the publisher for rectification.*

CONTENTS

WHO WERE THE SUMERIANS?

The Sumerians lived in Sumer, an ancient kingdom that occupied the land between the Tigris and Euphrates rivers in southern Mesopotamia, now modern Iraq. From 4500–4000 BCE, small settlements grew and by around 3500 BCE they had turned into large cities, marking the start of a unique civilisation. Each city state was like a separate country with its own king. Important city states included Ur, Akkad, Nippur, Lagash, Uruk, Kish and Eridu.

World firsts

The Sumerians were highly creative people who excelled at art and music, and made astonishing advances in farming, technology, writing, maths, astronomy and architecture. They invented many world 'firsts': the spoked wheel, a writing script, a code of law and systems of maths. From excavations led by archaeologist Leonard Woolley at Ur and Nippur in the 1920s and 1930s, we have a rich record of the wonderful objects and ideas left behind by the Sumerians.

This map shows the location of the important cities of the Sumer civilisation. Mesopotamia corresponds roughly to the area of modern-day Iraq.

5

This stele, or carved stone slab, was made by a prince of the city state of Lagash to celebrate a military victory over a rival city state in about 2450 BCE.

Lasting influence

In 2334 BCE, King Sargon of Akkad took control of all the Sumer city states. Even though King Ur-Nammu reclaimed Sumer lands in 2112 BCE, rebuilding cities and constructing ziggurats (see page 22) to honour the gods, his Third Dynasty of Ur was not to last. In 2004 BCE, Ur was destroyed by people from the nearby land of Elam. By 1900 BCE, the Amorite people had taken over Mesopotamia. Sumer merged with the new culture. But those that followed — the Babylonians and Assyrians — built empires based on the amazing achievements of the Sumerians.

SPECIAL CODE

The Code of Ur-Nammu is a set of laws that states how Sumerian people had to behave. It also divides Sumerian society into royalty, free people and slaves, each with a job to do — king, farmer, scribe, musician, scientist or craftsperson — as well as a role within the family.

6

Big wig

Among the many achievements of King Ur-Nammu (who reigned c. 2112–2095 BCE) was the creation of the world's first code of law. The Code of Ur-Nammu set out punishments for crimes such as murder, witchcraft or slander (speaking badly of someone). While some punishments were harsh, others simply involved paying a fine. Someone found guilty of murder or robbery could be put to death.

Cutting edge

Normally only wealthy boys went to school, studying subjects such as maths, music and writing. Students copied their lessons onto clay tablets and later had to recite them from memory to the headmaster – if they didn't remember, they might be caned! Some high-born girls studied as well, and became priestesses, scribes or musicians.

This stone tablet dates from c. 2095 BCE and records the laws from the Code of Ur-Nammu.

7

This detail from the stele of Ur-Nammu shows King Ur-Nammu making an offering to the moon god Nanna and dates from c. 2060 BCE.

Family life

Having many children — especially boys — was very important to the Sumerians, so that the young could grow up and work for the family farm or business. Girls married in their teens and were given a dowry, a gift that could include land and slaves, for the husband's family. The groom in turn would bring a ring, silver or clothing to the bride's family. Divorce was allowed but frowned upon.

Around the world

c. 3050–350 BCE Egypt
Society is made up of many levels, but men and women from all classes are equal under the law, except slaves.

450 BCE Europe
The laws of the Twelve Tables set down the basis for Roman law, which grows with the Roman Empire. Many of its legal terms are still used today.

c. 9th–15th century CE Europe
A feudal society operates, with land-owning lords, vassals, who were the tenants, and peasants who worked the land.

A SUMERIAN SHEPHERD

Sumerian shepherds led a semi-nomadic life like their ancestors, moving their herds of sheep with the seasons. In winter, they lived in the valleys, while during summer, they would climb high up the mountainsides. Farmers who tended the land invented many ways to help grow crops and raise animals. The produce from their farms provided food for people both in the villages and the cities.

Archaeologists discovered this terracotta statue of a Sumerian shepherd with a lamb in Girsu. It dates from between 3000 and 2000 BCE.

8

A modern photo shows stalks of an ancient grain called einkorn, an important staple crop in Sumer for thousands of years.

Flesh, fish and fowl

Farmers in Sumer domesticated goats from about 8000 BCE, and tamed sheep and cattle later on. The animals were used for milk, meat, hides (leather) and wool. Farmers kept geese and ducks for their eggs and meat, and hunted fallow deer. Fish from rivers added another important food to people's diet.

Growing strong

The Sumerians grew vegetables such as peas and beans, onions and garlic, and enjoyed fruit including figs, dates, pomegranates and grapes. Farmers used ploughs pulled by oxen and worked out how to channel water from the Tigris and Euphrates rivers to the fields, to water their crops. Farmers became so successful in growing food that this allowed cities to grow. In the cities people developed skills in writing and crafts.

Cutting edge

Sumerian farmers also cultivated wild varieties of cereal grains. They chose those with the largest seedheads to plant, so over time the plants became larger and easier to harvest. They grew einkorn and emmer, ancient varieties of the wheat we use today to make bread. Emmer became the most important grain crop for thousands of years.

Around the world

2700 BCE Central America
Corn or maize is grown as a crop in Mesoamerica. It later becomes the staple food for many cultures.

1900 BCE Middle East
The first aqueducts in the world are constructed on Minoan Crete and in Mesopotamia.

1500 BCE Asia
Growing crops in fields begins across the Eurasian steppes, later spreading across the world.

RICH HEADDRESS

Archaeologists were startled to discover a huge amount of jewellery in the tomb of Queen Puabi in Ur. Perhaps the most amazing piece is her stunning gold and lapis lazuli headdress, truly fit for a queen. An abundance of necklaces, rings and bracelets was also found next to her skeleton.

10

Cutting edge

Women wore kohl – a black powder – around their eyes. They may have also used eye shadow: shells with pigments in many colours have been found, as well as a make-up case made of gold and silver. Perfumes made from the essence of flowers and resins, such as myrrh, were popular.

The headdress of Queen Puabi consists of gold leaves and flowers made of precious stones. It dates from c. 2550 BCE.

Dazzling jewellery

The playful and creative design of Queen Puabi's
headdress makes it one of the most unique pieces
of jewellery in the ancient world. It consists of lapis
lazuli bands and beads, layers of gold rings, and rows
of gold leaves with carnelian beads. Lapis lazuli, silver
and golden rings and bracelets were also found, as well as
decorated gold hair combs and hooped earrings. In Sumer,
men, women and children all wore jewellery.

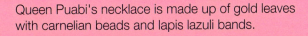

Queen Puabi's necklace is made up of gold leaves
with carnelian beads and lapis lazuli bands.

Sumer fashions

Clay tablets and plaques show Sumerian women wearing
sheepskin or woollen dresses that left one shoulder bare.
They also wore woollen cloaks. Men wore sheepskin kilts,
often leaving their chests bare. Hairstyles varied: in earlier
dynasties, women wore their hair long and men shaved
theirs, but during the Akkadian era, some men had long,
wavy hair – just like their king!

11

 ## Around the world

c. 3000 BCE Egypt
The Egyptians were using
electrum – an alloy of gold
and silver.

c. 1600–1046 BCE China
Wealthy people during
the Shang Dynasty wear
necklaces, bracelets and
rings made from jade.

c. 800–700 BCE Europe
Gold workers in Ireland
craft gold collars to wear
as jewellery, including the
Shannongrove Gorget.

MODEL CHARIOT

Sometime around 3500 BCE, the Sumerians became one of the first groups of people to use the wheel. At first it was used on simple sleds to transport people and heavy goods for trade. Later, wheeled war chariots were used by armies in battle.

Land routes

The chariot started out as a slow, heavy vehicle with solid, circular wheels. With the invention of spoked wheels around 2000 BCE, travel became lighter and faster. Roads were also constructed around this time. When a new road was built from Ur to Nippur, King Shulgi of Ur (2094–2047 BCE) is said to have run back and forth between the cities (320 km) in two days, stopping halfway for a banquet and a few hours' sleep!

12

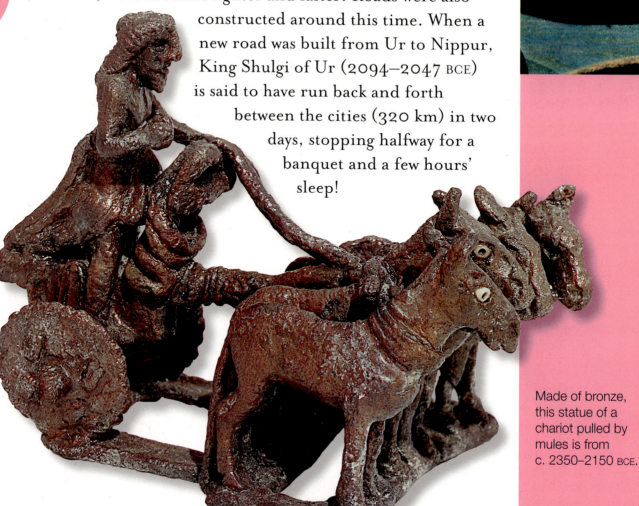

Made of bronze, this statue of a chariot pulled by mules is from c. 2350–2150 BCE.

The quffa – shown here in a photo from 1900 – was used as a fishing boat in Sumer.

Water transport

Sumerians used a small, round boat called a *quffa* – similar to the coracle – to travel on the river. The quffa was made of woven reeds covered with bitumen, a type of tar, which waterproofed the boat. Sailing boats were invented as early as 4000–3500 BCE, making it faster to trade goods with people in far-away lands.

13

Cutting edge

A vast number of sloped rim bowls have been found across all of Mesopotamia. These thick clay containers were made in Uruk, and were used to dish out grain and oil to pay labourers for their work. The bowls are thought to be the first mass-produced products in history.

Around the world

16th century BCE Egypt
Hyksos invaders introduce the wheeled chariot to Egypt, contributing to Egyptian military success.

1st century BCE Europe
The Romans use sprung wagons for overland journeys and to help rule the Roman Empire.

c. 1200 BCE China
Chariots are used during the Shang Dynasty using technology that may have come from the Caucasus or Central Asia.

SILVER LYRE

One of the most beautiful artefacts found in the Sumerian royal tombs is the silver lyre, a large stringed instrument. From the number of musical objects found by archaeologists, we know that the Sumerians had a deep love of music. They were also skilled artists, producing the stunning Standard of Ur – shown on the right.

14

Standing a metre high, the lyre of Ur is made from wood, silver, shell and precious stones. It dates from c. 2600–2400 BCE.

Bull song

The lyre of Ur has a silver frame and a wooden soundbox decorated with a bull's head. When played, it may have sounded like a cello. Drums, flutes, cymbals and clay pipes were played at festivals and religious rites. A beautiful harp found in Queen Puabi's tomb would have sounded like a guitar.

Cutting edge

A scale with seven notes – like the white keys on a piano – was played on the lyre, but the instrument did not have half steps (like black piano keys). Sumerian music used seven scales, one of which sounds the same as our modern major scale! This music system became popular with other cultures, and was used as far away as the Mediterranean.

Mystery box

Dating from about 2600 BCE, the Standard of Ur is a unique wooden box inlaid with mosaic pictures. On this side (see above) is a Sumerian army with chariots and prisoners of war; the reverse shows a banquet scene and animals. When it was first discovered, historians thought that it was carried on a pole to lead soldiers into war but now most people agree that we don't know how it was used. The materials used to make the box prove that the Sumerians were trading goods far and wide and were able to make things of great beauty.

The 'war' side of the Standard of Ur shows a Sumerian army and its chariots with prisoners of war on the top right. It dates from c. 2600 BCE.

 ## Around the world

2000 BCE Egypt
The first lyre (a stringed instrument) is played with a plectrum.

c. 600 BCE Europe
Sculpture becomes one of the most important forms of art for the Greeks, influencing the Romans and many other cultures.

c. 600 BCE Europe
A complex music theory evolves, including the notes and intervals of different musical scales.

CLAY SCRIPT

The Sumerians invented a system of writing in around 3100 BCE at Uruk. The first writing was made up of pictograms (pictures that represent words) to record information about practical things such as crops and taxes. Eventually, the symbols developed into a script called cuneiform.

16

This tablet clearly shows how Sumerian scribes used a triangular stylus (writing tool) to impress characters on the surface of wet clay.

Impressions

The Sumerians didn't have paper. Instead, they formed tablets from damp clay and used a stylus (reed) to make impressions on the surface. The tablets were baked hard in a kiln (hot oven). Cuneiform 'letters' were wedge-shaped and represented ideas as well as words. Over 600 signs were used, making it possible to write down laws, scientific texts, historical records – and even story books!

17

This cylinder seal and its clay impression belonged to a governor of Nippur, once a religious centre in Sumer. It dates from around 2500 BCE.

Signed and sealed

Signature seals were used by rulers, priests and other important people to 'sign' their names and mark property. The seal was a stone cylinder, carved with scenes and symbols that represented its owner. The owner pressed and rolled the seal onto a damp clay tablet to create a unique picture. When a person died, he or she was buried with their seal.

 ## Around the world

1850–1400 BCE Aegean
The Minoan civilisation invents Cretan script, a hieroglyphic script that has not yet been deciphered.

1000 BCE Greece
The Greek alphabet appears, and eventually becomes the root of all modern European alphabets.

c. 647–c. 627 BCE Middle East
A large collection of clay tablets called Ashurbanipal's Library is put together at Nineveh (now Mosul, Iraq).

MATHS CHIP

The Sumerians began writing down numbers over 5,000 years ago. They invented a system of maths based on the number 60, and they also used a decimal system based on the number 10. As with writing words, calculations were worked out on clay tablets. This system worked hand-in-hand with astronomy and led to great advances in timekeeping.

A clay tablet shows 14 lines of maths text in cuneiform, with a geometric design, from Mesopotamia.

Starry-eyed

Sumerian astronomers studied the stars and the movement of the Sun, Moon and planets across the night sky. They used this information to predict the future, and also to keep track of the seasons, vital for working out the best time to plant crops. Carved onto one cylinder seal dating from 4,500 years ago is what looks to be a map of the solar system, with the Sun and planets!

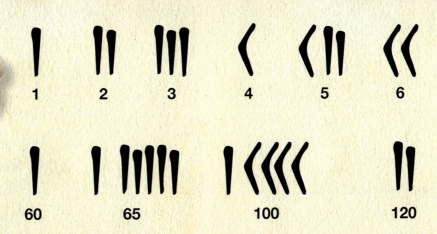

| 1 | 2 | 3 | 4 | 5 | 6 |

| 60 | 65 | 100 | 120 |

A selection of symbols from the Sumerian mathematical system.

Cutting edge

To write down numbers, Sumerian mathematicians pressed a stylus into a wet clay tablet, making wedge-shaped marks. The symbol for '1' and '60' were the same, as the number base was 60. There was no symbol for '0'. Remembering things such as multiplication tables must have been tricky, so these were pressed into clay tablets so that people could look them up.

Touching base

Astronomers worked out a calendar that was based on 12- and 28-day cycles, which used a week with seven days. The Sumer were also the first to divide an hour into 60 minutes and a circle into 360 degrees. Today, we still use some of the Sumerians' concepts in geometry and calendars.

Around the world

**c. 5th century BCE
Central America**
The Maya develop the Long Count Calendar, based on a ritual cycle of 260 named days and a year made up of 365 days.

450 BCE Greece
The parapegma star calendar is created by Meton and Euctemon. This tracked the movement of the stars and constellations.

c. 390 CE Greece
Hypatia becomes a leading teacher of mathematics at the University of Alexandria. She also taught astronomy and philosophy.

GOLDEN RAM

Some archaeologists believe this figure is a ram, others think it is a goat. Everyone agrees the statuette shows what expert craftspeople the Sumerians were. Other objects, such as bronze and pottery vessels, tell the story of their advanced technology in metalworking and pottery.

20

Ram on

The cheerful 'Ram in a Thicket' statuette dates from 2600-2400 BCE. Its head and legs are covered in gold leaf, while its fleece is made from lapis lazuli and shell. Craftsmen shaped the delicate golden flowers that spring out from a gold-leaf covered tree. Each step of making the figure would have taken a great deal of skill.

Archaeologist Leonard Woolley discovered a pair of these ram statuettes at Ur in the 1920s. One is in the British Museum, London, the other is in the University of Pennsylvania Museum in Philadelphia, USA.

Techy types

The Sumerians developed technologies to use different materials early in their history. At first, they moulded clay by hand to make pottery. Then in around 3500 BCE, they invented the potter's wheel, which made it easier to produce cups and bowls. They used the kiln (hot oven) to fire (or harden) wet clay objects, which were often painted with intricate designs.

This stunning golden goblet was found in the tomb of Queen Puabi in Ur and dates from 2600–2400 BCE.

Cutting edge

Early in their history, the Sumerians made objects such as weapons and tools from copper. But by about 3000 BCE, the Sumerians had discovered how to make a stronger metal, bronze, an alloy of copper and tin. Elegant tableware such as fluted bronze bowls, jugs and drinking goblets have all been found in the royal tombs. These were probably made for use in religious rituals.

21

 ## Around the world

c. 2500 BCE Egypt
The Egyptians invent a technique to create filigree – fine metal wire worked into a design – for making gold objects.

c. 2000 BCE Greece
The pottery wheel is introduced on Minoan Crete, to help produce bowls and cups and food vessels.

900 BCE Greece
Potters create a geometric design of regular lines and shapes.

ZIGGURAT OF UR

In around 2100 BCE, the Ziggurat of Ur — a vast building at the heart of the city of Ur — was built by King Ur-Nammu. Its clever design and huge size rival the pyramids built by the ancient Egyptians. Later, ziggurats were built in other city states.

22

The Ziggurat of Ur was excavated in the 1920s and 1930s and then partly restored by the Iraqi government during the 1980s.

Towering temple

Archaeologists believe that the Ziggurat of Ur was a temple dedicated to the moon god Nanna. Almost seven million mud bricks weighing up to 15 kg each were used in the first stage of construction, each stamped with the name 'Ur-Nammu'. The ziggurat had terraces at different levels, reached by a series of staircases, and at the top, a temple where only priests were allowed. The ziggurat was the home of the gods on Earth, and so it was a sacred place.

The ruins of the temple of Anu can be seen at the site of Uruk, one of the biggest cities in the ancient kingdom of Sumer.

Muddy homes

The houses of ordinary people in Sumer were also made of mud bricks, which were moulded from wet clay and straw, then left to harden in the sunshine. Some dwellings were two stories high and shared a wall with a neighbour, rather like modern terraced houses. The top floor was open to the sky. People used it for cooking and for sleeping outside on hot nights.

23

Cutting edge

Uruk is thought to be the earliest city in all of Mesopotamia. At its height around 3000 BCE, it was the largest and most powerful urban area in Sumer. Dedicated to the goddess Inanna and the sky god Anu, Uruk was a centre of culture and invention: the first writing, signature seals and stone building work all developed here.

 ## Around the world

2575 BCE Egypt
Construction begins on the Great Pyramid of Giza, the largest pyramid ever built.

c. 1300 BCE China
The Chinese trade centre of Anyang becomes the capital of the Shang Dynasty.

2 CE Central America
Building starts on the Pyramids of the Sun and Moon in central Mexico by a mysterious people who came before the Maya.

A ROYAL GAME

When a board game was found in a royal tomb at Ur, archaeologists were amazed at its beauty — and were intrigued to know how to play the game. Other objects, such as dice and plaques, give us clues about pastimes and sports the Sumerians enjoyed.

Gorgeous game

The Royal Game of Ur is the oldest board game ever found. Crafted from wood and bitumen, the board was embedded with colourful lapis lazuli, shell, pink limestone and red glass. Players raced their seven counters along a path to reach the finish line, knocking off the opponent's counters along the way.

24

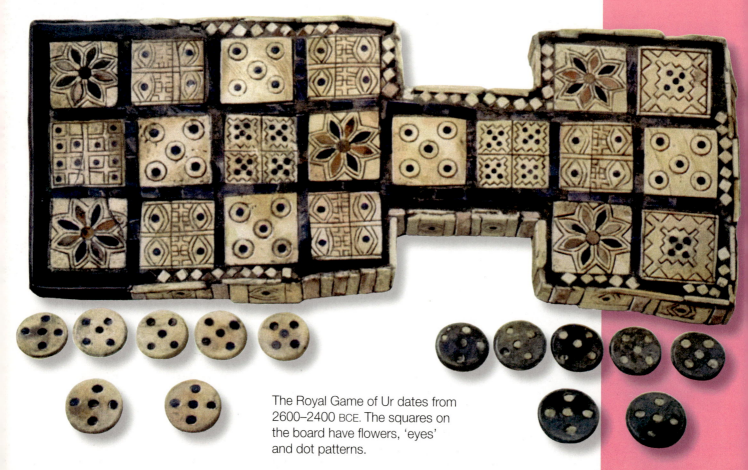

The Royal Game of Ur dates from 2600–2400 BCE. The squares on the board have flowers, 'eyes' and dot patterns.

Keeping fit

The Sumerians took part in sporting games, too. Sport contests, such as wrestling and boxing, were common in Sumer. A 4,000-year-old terracotta plaque showing two men boxing was found in Eshnunna — the earliest ever picture of a match! With temperatures sometimes reaching 40°C in summer, children and adults cooled off by swimming in the river.

25

Found at Eshnunna, another Sumerian city state, this terracotta plaque shows a boxing match that took place c. 2000 BCE. Neither man is wearing boxing gloves.

Cutting edge

The world's most ancient dice – made in around 2750 BCE – were found in the ruins of the Mesopotamian city of Tepe Gawra. Gambling games were also played with sticks and discs.

Around the world

c. 850 BCE Central America
The Maya use a large stone court at Chichen Itza to play a ritual ball game called pok-a-tok, the world's oldest-known team sport.

Before 776 BCE Greece
First record of foot races being held every four years in Olympia, Greece. These were probably the first Olympic Games.

618 BCE China
Polo is played by both noble men and women of the Tang Dynasty, China.

MOON GOD

The Sumerians worshipped hundreds of gods and goddesses, who were thought to be like humans, but had a god-like aura or glow. Each city state was dedicated to a particular god that protected its citizens. In return, people offered gifts of food and wine at the god's temple. The moon god, Nanna, was important to all Sumerians.

26

This relief shows the crescent moon of Nanna, god of the Moon, and the symbol for the sun god Shamash c. 2000 BCE.

Top gods

Enlil was the father of many gods and goddesses, and protected the city of Nippur. He was said to be so powerful that the other gods were not allowed to look at him. Inanna (or Ishtar) was the goddess of love and war, governing both marriage and battle. In a sacred ceremony held each year, she 'married' the king. Her domain in the sky was the planet Venus.

A detail from this vase shows men making offerings to Inanna, goddess of love and war. It is from Uruk and dates from c. 3000 BCE.

Dusty afterlife

Belief in an afterlife was crucial to the Sumerians. Called 'The Land of No Return', their underworld was a shadowy place of sadness. Here, the winged souls of the dead ate dust. Most Sumerians were buried in clay coffins, sometimes placed under the courtyard of family homes. Only royalty and high-born nobles were buried in extravagant tombs.

Cutting edge

Around 1,800 graves were found at the Royal Tombs of Ur, most of them belonging to ordinary people. However, 17 burials were special – and Queen Puabi's tomb was the most breathtaking of all. Not only was it crammed with treasure, but the skeletons of ten handmaidens and five guards surrounded her body. Puabi's servants had been sacrificed to serve their queen in the afterlife.

27

This 1st century clay coffin from Uruk is similar to the coffins ordinary people were buried in during ancient Sumer times.

Around the world

c. 4000 BCE Europe
Burials begin at the passage tombs of Carrowmore Megalithic Cemetery in Sligo, Ireland.

c. 1323 BCE Egypt
Pharaoh Tutankhamun's mummy is laid in a gold sarcophagus. His tomb walls show pictures of the gods and afterlife.

c. 1200 BCE China
Warrior queen Fu Hao is buried in a tomb stuffed with treasures, chariots and dead servants during the Shang Dynasty.

KING'S HELMET

As Sumerian city states grew larger, more land, food, water and timber were needed to support growing populations, and cities were constantly at war with each other. Sophisticated armour and weaponry – such as helmets, daggers and chariots – were developed to help drive a state to victory.

28

This gold ceremonial helmet dates from c. 2400 BCE and was found inside the tomb of King Meskalamdug.

Golden head

The finely crafted gold and silver helmet of King Meskalamdug, an early ruler of Ur, was probably made for ceremonial use – gold is a soft metal and would not have protected his head from blows. But its design shows how serious the Sumer were about war. Copper or leather helmets were used in battle, along with stiff leather cloaks to protect the body and leather shields to fend off blows from spears.

Lethal weapons

Weapons used by Sumerian soldiers included copper daggers and battle axes. In early times, heavy war wagons carrying supplies were pulled by asses. Later, wagons were replaced by lighter horse-drawn chariots, making warfare more swift and lethal.

A dagger excavated at Ur would have struck a lethal blow to Sumerian enemies. It probably dates from 2600–2400 BCE.

29

Cutting edge

King Sargon of Akkad was a ruthless military leader who waged war against Sumer city states in the 24th century BCE. He was so successful that he conquered all of Sumer and founded an empire, reigning from about 2334–2279 BCE. The Akkadian Empire lasted only about 150 years, but had its own language. Even after the Sumerians regained control during the Third Dynasty of Ur (2112–2004 BCE), Akkadian continued to be the spoken and written language.

 Around the world

c. 1178 BCE Egypt
Pharaoh Ramesses III defeats the Sea Peoples on the shores of Xois, a city in the Nile Delta.

c. 1258 BCE Egypt
The world's first peace treaty – the Treaty of Kadesh – is made between the Egyptians and the Hittites.

1000 BCE Europe
In ancient Britain, swords are used for warfare and also thrown in rivers as offerings to the gods.

GLOSSARY

alloy A metal made by mixing two or more metallic elements, usually to make it stronger.

ancestors Generations of people from whom a person is descended.

archaeologist A person who studies human history through places and objects left behind.

astronomer Someone who studies the movement of the Sun, Moon, stars and planets.

bitumen A sticky black substance used to waterproof an object or surface a road.

carnelian A pale red or reddish-white semi-precious stone.

city state A city that functions as a separate country, with its own king or queen and the surrounding lands.

copper A reddish-brown coloured metal.

cuneiform An ancient writing script with wedge-shaped characters, used in Mesopotamia.

domesticated Refers to an animal that has been tamed to be kept for farm work or as a pet.

dowry Property, goods or money given by a bride to her new husband.

einkorn and emmer Ancient types of wheat grown in the Sumer region.

gold leaf A very thin sheet of gold used to cover an object, often a piece of art or jewellery.

irrigation A system of watering crops, using channels, in a dry land or during a dry season

jade A hard green stone.

kohl A black powder used as eye make-up.

lapis lazuli A bright blue rock used in jewellery and to decorate objects.

lyre A stringed instrument common in Sumer and ancient Greece.

Mesopotamia An ancient area in present-day Iraq, between the Tigris and Euphrates rivers. It was home to ancient civilisations including Sumer, Akkad, Babylonia and Assyria.

mud bricks Bricks made from baked mud.

pictogram A picture symbol for a word or phrase.

potter's wheel A rotating disc on which clay is shaped into cups, bowls and pots.

semi-nomadic Travelling from place to place to live for part of the year.

standard A ceremonial flag or object carried on a pole.

ziggurat A tower made up of different stepped levels with a temple at the top.

30

WEBSITES

https://youtu.be/VroX-_thMLg
Watch a video showing how the Sumerians wrote cuneiform on clay tablets and hear stories from *The Epic of Gilgamesh.*

http://m.youtube.com/watch?v=2H8_13x3JaI
http://m.youtube.com/watch?v=6dVQqtlbPPo
Listen to ancient Sumerian music for lyres, flutes and other instruments, played by modern-day musicians.

http://www.mesopotamia.co.uk/menu.html
Find out how ziggurats were built, learn about Sumerian gods and goddesses, and explore how the Royal Tombs of Ur were discovered in this fascinating, interactive site from the British Museum.

http://mesopotamia.mrdonn.org/sumer.html
Discover amazing facts about Sumerian religion, music, warfare and more. The site includes fun Sumerian and Mesopotamian clip art.

http://www.bbc.co.uk/schools/primaryhistory/worldhistory/royal_game_of_ur/
Learn how to play the Royal Game of Ur board game on the BBC's fascinating site.

Note to parents and teachers
Every effort has been made by the Publishers to ensure that the websites in this book are suitable for children, that they are of the highest educational value, and that they contain no inappropriate or offensive material. However, because of the nature of the Internet, it is impossible to guarantee that the contents of these sites will not be altered. We strongly advise that Internet access is supervised by a responsible adult.

TIMELINE

7000 BCE The first peoples begin to live in the Mesopotamian region.

c. 4500-4000 BCE Small settlements begin to develop and grow in size.

c. 3500 BCE The first city states develop in Sumer, including Ur, Nippur, Uruk, Lagash and Kish.

c. 3500 BCE Sumerians begin to use the wheel on sledges; the potter's wheel is invented to shape clay into pottery cups, bowls and objects.

c. 3100 BCE Cuneiform writing develops, probably at Uruk in Sumer.

c. 3000 BCE Uruk is the largest city state in Mesopotamia, becoming the most powerful metropolis by 2500 BCE.

2900–2330 BCE The Early Dynastic Period in Sumer.

c. 2600-2400 BCE Queen Puabi is buried with her servants at Ur, a wealthy city state.

c. 2334 BCE King Sargon of Akkad (reigned 2334–2279 BCE) conquers all of Sumer and founds the Akkadian Empire.

2112 BCE King Ur-Nammu of Ur reclaims the Sumerian city states; beginning of the Third Dynasty of Ur. He rebuilds old cities and constructs the Ziggurat of Ur. The Third Dynasty ends in around 2004 BCE.

c. 1900 BCE The Amorite people conquer all of Mesopotamia, and the Sumer civilisation merges with other cultures.

31

INDEX

32